Inside My Head

Alicia Doyle

Presentation by *BookLeaf Publishing*

Web: www.bookleafpub.com

E-mail: info@bookleafpub.com

ISBN: 9789357612180

First edition 2021

To my little sister, Sam. You are the bravest and
the strongest person I know.

ACKNOWLEDGEMENT

I really want to thank my husband and children who allowed me the time to write and some of the inspiration.

PREFACE

This is my first official written work. The poems are a reflection of the mood I was in when I wrote them. Writing them was eye opening and confirmed for me that I want to be an author. Some days, it was a challenge to write even a couple of lines, but completing this reinforced that as long as you never give up, even one step in the right direction you can live your dreams. This book is proof for me that I can do amazing things. I hope you enjoy.

The Dark Within

Way down deep; the dark within,
Where soul and essence sleep,
A sly and ever mighty foe,
Nefarious it creeps.
With vise-like grip, it sinks its claws
It tears apart its host.
Invisible to all outside,
Intangible; A ghost,
That haunts in waking, and in dreams
Escape or fight, or medicate
"Save yourself," the world cries out,
Though resources, won't dedicate.
"Smile," "cheer up," "it's not so bad"
The empty words so freely fall
As if you hadn't thought of that,
It makes one feel so small.
Helpless, hopeless, at wit's end,
Hanging on, but by a thread.
It feels so real, I can't believe
It's all just in my head.

Choices

The choices we make,
After thought, or by whim,
The ripples of consequence plain,
Determine our path
And the life that we live,
Though we try to deny it in vain.

Our choices will follow us,
Define who we are,
In all that we say and do.
But by what measure?
For good or for ill?
Will they benefit many or few?

You only live once,
At least that's what they say.
The decisions you make are your own.
Make them firmly and thoughtfully,
Open-minded, and free,
And embrace the exciting unknown.

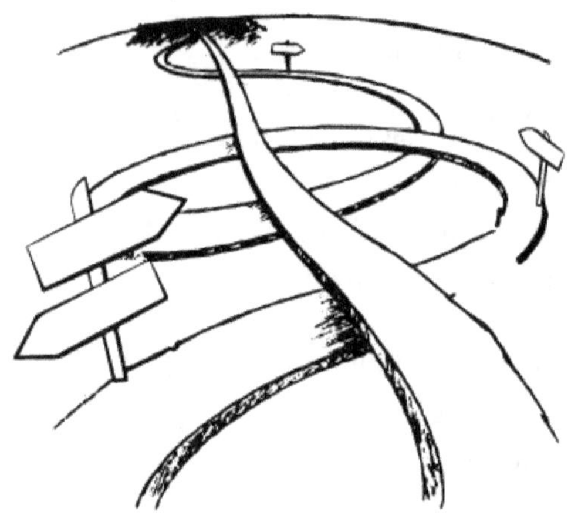

The Spark

Words have power, words have weight
Both to destroy and to create
In every language on this earth
Though they vary, words have worth

Some are beautiful, others plain
Bring great joy or sometimes pain
Whatever purpose, think it through
The words you choose reflect on you

When tossed around without a care
The impact of which, we're unaware
Used without thought, consider this
Intent will surely be amiss

So, use your words to bring forth light
Lift others up with all your might
Words can be magic, dispel the dark
In the heart of another, let your words be the
spark

Cancel Culture

The Power to Speak or to act as you please
To think what you like, to object, disagree
We thought they were freedoms, protected and
safe,
Then the "woke" in society started to chafe.

You cannot use this word, no, not even that.
Don't try to explain, it'll only fall flat.
It's just your opinion, don't try to quote facts.
The narrative meant to divide and distract.

What happened to justice? What happened to
truth?
If I don't play along, will you use it as proof?
That something within me just must be wrong
Does it make me evil if I don't play along?

When government moves to implement laws
And society panics because they have flaws,
Where are the heroes that can save the day?
I don't know, they've been cancel-cultured
away.

Insomnia

Late at night, when I can't sleep
I lay there, darkness all around
The thoughts are endless, unrelenting
I long to scream, but make no sound

Dear insomnia, my old friend
Why do you seem to vex me now
I feel exhausted, oh so weary
I'm still awake; I don't know how

To dreamless sleep I long to go
For dreaming brings me no delight
My own subconscious does betray
With dreams it conjures up at night

Oh sleep, I long for your embrace
Please let me in the darkness rest
With pleasant dreams and on my waking
I will give the world my best

Only Human

To admit I'm only human
Is harder than it seems
For if I do, I must accept
The truth of what it means

It means that I'm not perfect
I'm not really in control
That I must admit my weakness
That I might not reach my goal

I'm not the perfect parent,
Perfect friend, or perfect wife
I haven't found my calling
Or my purpose in this life

If I accept I'm only human
That I cannot do it all
Will I still feel like I'm worthy,
Raise my chin and stand up tall?

Can I be a good example?
If I'm not always at my best,
If I struggle, will my character
Withstand so tough a test?

To admit I'm only human,

Means accepting me for me
That I must let go and just embrace
My flawed humanity

Autumn

Endings can be beautiful,
The autumn leaves declare
As they paint the trees with colors
And a coolness chills the air

Crimson red, sunshine gold
And fire orange hues
The signs of seasons changing
Such as frosty morning dew

Apple cider, pumpkin pie
Turkey and harvest delights
I'm glad to exchange Summer days
For lovely, starry Autumn nights

The Summer heat is over
And Winter's cold is yet to be
I think that in her wisdom
Mother Nature made it just for me

Legacy

To the ones who walked before me
Are you proud of what you see?
Have I become what fate had planned?
Will I fulfill my destiny?

Is there some great purpose
Or a plan that is in place?
Will I live a life that's meaningful?
What challenges am I to face?

This life is rarely easy
And I know that's meant to be
Because anything that's worth it
Has a cost, it isn't free

I hope to make a difference
And to leave a legacy
I want to live a life that's worthy
Becoming what I'm meant to be

Your Love

The first face I am looking for
When I am in a crowd
The voice I long and listen for
When the world gets loud

Arms that hold and keep me safe
When I feel I'll break apart
Hands that know me expertly
Like you're the artist and I'm the art

When my mind is full of darkness
And I feel like I have gone astray
You are the light that calls me back
Your love is that which guides the way

#MomLife

Being a Mom is often hard
Though worth the struggle all the same
The hugs and snuggles are a joy...
Why can't they just forget my name

Mom, Mommy, Mama
Seems like all they ever say
As though Daddy were a stranger
Or he's only there come time to play

They run about and make a mess
With tiny hands and little feet
So full of life and energy
They always seem to want to eat

I look into their little faces
Smiles that warm and melt my heart
I love them more than life itself
They are my greatest work of art

Almost bedtime, I can't wait
The day's been long, and I am tired
I tuck them in, we say their prayers
But they're not sleepy, they are wired

And when they finally fall asleep

And quiet in the house descends
Into their rooms I softly creep
And watch my little hooligans

They grow so fast,
Please, Time, slow down
I am not ready to set them free
I hope they grow and always know
That welcome home, they'll always be

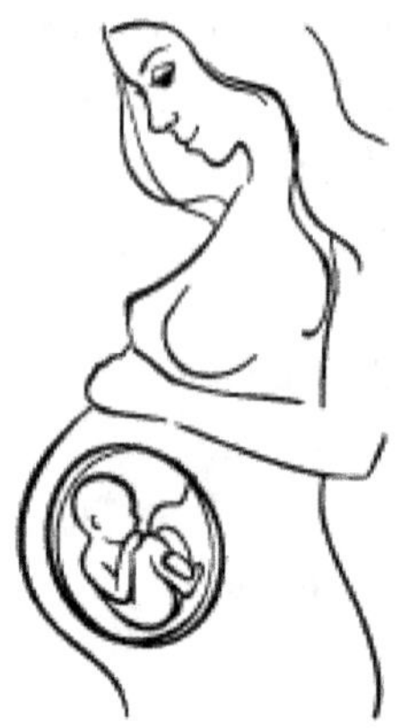

Grandma

She would drink coffee
And I would drink tea
We enjoyed spending time
Sometimes hours, her and me

Whether telling old stories
Or discussing what's new
My time spent with Grandma
Brought me joy through and through

She was thoughtful and funny
And her jokes were the best
She could bake like no other,
Oh, how we were blessed

Not a single day passes
When I don't wish to be
Spending more time with Grandma
Drinking coffee and tea

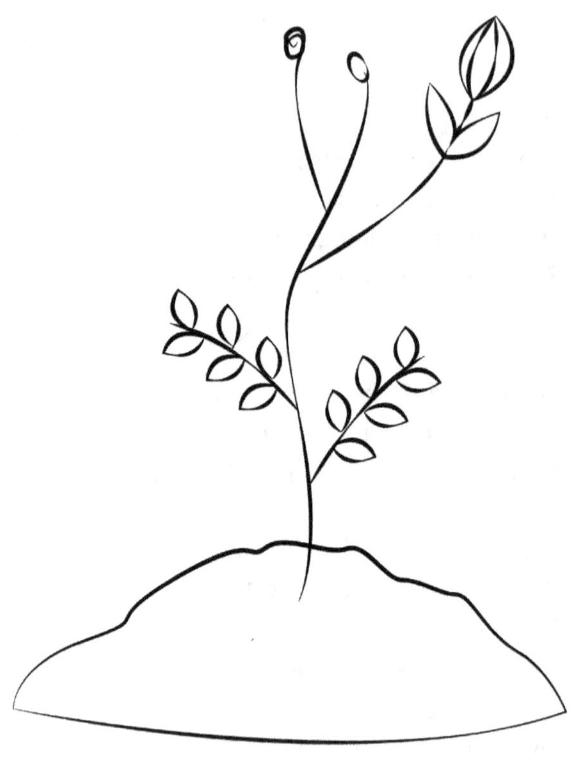

Magic Brought to Life

There is magic in the written word
Those ink and paper works of art
They weave the tales we love to hear
And find their way into our heart

They give a glimpse into the mind
Of someone else through space and time
The wisdom of the ages
Found between the many pages

Whether grounded in reality
Or rich with make-believe
The things we read will change us
There's no telling what we can achieve

The reader lives so many lives
The words are magic brought to life
In the pages of our stories
Is escape from pain and strife

So, if you're looking for adventure
Or have something new to learn
Try the pages of a book, my friend
There's no telling what you might upturn

Meant to be Here

I have never felt I'm normal
So, I learned to hate the word
After all, who says what's normal?
Random perspective? That's absurd!

It makes people who are perfect
As they are, feel like they're wrong
When the truth is our uniqueness
Is what makes us all belong

If everyone was all the same
No differences to find
Then what would make us beautiful?
Sadly, nothing comes to mind

Who we love, and where we live,
The beliefs that we hold dear
Are the parts that make life worth it
Just embrace it, don't spread fear

That uniqueness will not hurt you
Just let others live their truth
Be accepting without judgement
Lift them up, don't be uncouth

If you find that you don't understand

Don't give in to fear
Ask your questions, and be open
Lastly, please let me be clear

This does not mean you must agree
With everything you see or hear
But it's not your job to change them
We are all meant to be here.

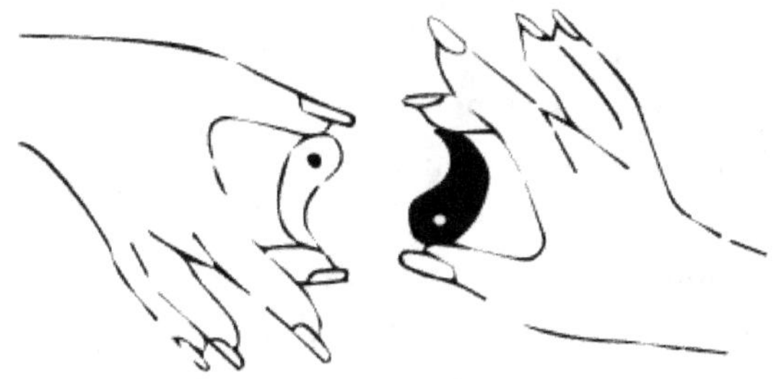

Tea

O' Steamy Cup of Therapy
My soul, in your warmth does delight
A welcome morning visitor
A soothing ritual at night

O' liquid wisdom I embrace
And relaxation that's diffused
Your steeping strength a gift
Providing clarity to minds confused

O' Delicious Leaf, Elixir from on High
Your varied forms and tastes adored
Accompanied by something sweet
In comfy chair with written word

The calming nectar, steeped to heal
Troubled mind and weary flesh
With reverence and full of zeal
I will consume until my death

The Real Me

Will I remember the real me
When my children have all grown?
Will I recognize myself
Without the roles that I have known?

Sometimes when I look in the mirror
It's just a stranger that I see.
Who am I underneath the load
Of my responsibility?

I am more than all the labels
I am more than just the hats I wear
And without a grasp of the real me
Sometimes I'm filled with such despair.

I know time passes quickly
Even though the days drag on,
So I hope someday I'll find
I've known the real me all along.

Little Boys

Little Boys are made of magic
And they fill my heart with such delight
From the time their feet first hit the floor
Until they fall asleep at night

They are balls of endless energy
Those mess and noise machines
But when they sleep, they look like angels
They are less wild than the daylight makes them
seem

They climb and run and break things
Yet their hugs and kisses melt your heart
To keep them safe and happy
As their mom, you'd tear the world apart

You hope they grow up strong and brave
That they will live to do what's right
Men of honour and of Virtue
That in darkness they will be a light

But for now, they are still little
Please love and mold them as they grow
Take tender care to plant the seeds
The world will reap that which we sow

Nature's Power

Somewhere in the distance
Lightning rips apart the sky
As the thunder rumbles deeply
In a well rehearsed reply

The clouds are dark and threaten rain
The winds send detritus askew
Nature's power on full display
Her Majesty in perfect view

A dragonfly, a snowflake
A flower that is in full bloom
The power that creates the storm
Knits us together in the womb

A balance that's so perfect
A flawless mastery that's not impugned
Destruction and Creation's dance
A Universe completely attuned

Universal Language

It's a universal language
That is written on ours hearts
It's the sounds and words that speak to us
An interactive work of art

From the moment we are born on earth
It is music that accompanies life
Beginning with our hearts own beat
A constant through both joy and strife

Perfect in its precision
Resonant and deep
Music whispers truth into our souls
Like a secret it can't bear to keep

It evokes in us emotion
Sometimes songs say what we cannot speak
So, if ever you are weary
Let music be the rest you seek

Cloudy Grey with Rosy Hue

Do you know the colour of the sky?
When sun sets amid the storm,
A cloudy grey with rosy hue?
Not quite happy or forlorn.

If a colour could define me
Then that's the one that I would choose
A shade that's close to cloudy grey
And tinged throughout with rosy hues.

You will not find complete darkness
But the ever-present threat of storm
And you'll marvel at that bit of light
And the wonders that it can perform

The light is love of friends and family
It is the spark of goals achieved
It is the things that we look forward to
It is the goodness given and received

It's the anchor holding fast and true
It is the lighthouse on a stormy sea
The parts that make our life worth living
And the purpose life has given me

A Test of Character

If you want to reveal character
Or take the measure of someone
You can start by giving power
And see the leader they become

Will they lead with understanding
And stand up for what is true?
Or will they take the power given to them
And be a tyrant through and through?

A second test, another way
To ascertain a temperament
Keep them from getting what they want
Their response will be the measurement

Will they rage and show their selfishness?
Or will they graciously accept their fate?
They will show you who they really are,
Are they flexible or obdurate?

You see, the nature of a person
Isn't always as it seems
People are changed each day by living
From their failures and their dreams

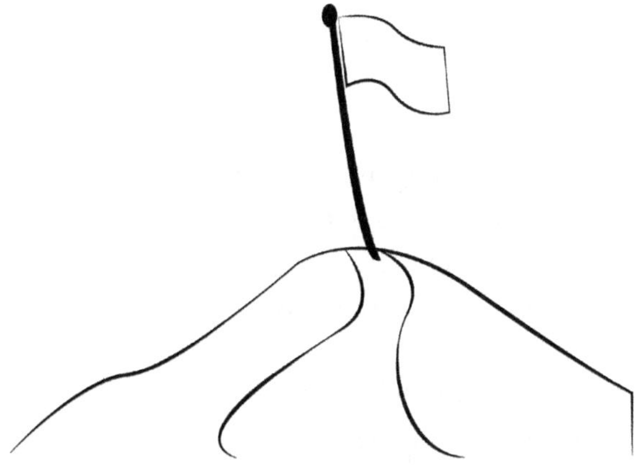

My Words

As I put my thoughts on paper
And the story starts to come alive
It feels like I'm performing magic
My creativity begins to thrive

I thought it would be easy
I thought it would be fun
But it is anything but easy
I know the fight to write will be hard won

It is more than just desire
But that's a perfect place to start
You will also need much discipline
If you want to create written art

It is the mountain I have chosen
I will embrace the challenge of the climb
Perhaps my words will be my legacy
And my writing stand the test of time

It is what I've always wanted
And I write for no one else but me
Although I hope to be an influence
And through my words have immortality